Like us Follow us Pin us Sign up for newsletters

Printed in Canada
ISBN #978-1-927484-05-0

1. Tri-Fold Tote (crochet)

1 4 MEDIUM INTERMEDIATE

MEASUREMENTS

Approx 18" [45.5 cm] wide x 18" [45.5 cm] high (excluding strap).

GAUGE

15 sc and 16 rows = 4" [10 cm].

MATERIALS

Bernat® Handicrafter® Cotton (50 g/1.75 oz; 73 m/80 yds)		
Contrast A Tangerine (13699)	**2 balls**	**135 m/148 yds**
Contrast B Robin's Egg (13215)	**3 balls**	**160 m/175 yds**
Contrast C Warm Brown (13130)	**2 balls**	**125 m/137 yds**
Contrast D Off White (00002)	**2 balls**	**105 m/115 yds**
Contrast E Hot Green (13712)	**2 balls**	**105 m/115 yds**

Size 4 mm (U.S. G/6) crochet hook **or size needed to obtain gauge.** 1 toggle.

ABBREVIATIONS

See page 41 for Helpful Hints.

Approx = Approximately
Beg = Beginning
Ch = Chain(s)
Dc = Double crochet
Dc2tog = (Yoh and draw up a loop in next stitch. Yoh and draw through 2 loops on hook) twice. Yoh and draw through all loops on hook.
Dcbp = Yoh and draw up a loop around post of next stitch at back of work, inserting hook from right to left. (Yoh and draw through 2 loops on hook) twice.
Dec = Decrease(ing)
Hdc = Half double crochet
Hdc2tog = (Yoh and draw up a loop in next stitch) twice. Yoh and draw through all loops on hook.
Inc = Increase(ing)
Rem = Remaining
Rep = Repeat
Rnd(s) = Round(s)
RS = Right side
Sc = Single crochet
Sl st = Slip stitch
Sp(s) = Space(s)
Sts = Stitch(es)
Tog = Together
WS = Wrong side
Yoh = Yarn over hook

INSTRUCTIONS

Motif (make 3)

(See Chart I on page 10).

Note: Ch 3 at beg of rnd counts as dc throughout.

To change colors, work to last 2 loops on hook of first color. Yoh with new color and draw through rem 2 loops and proceed.

With A, ch 4. Join with sl st to first ch to form a ring.

1st rnd: Ch 3. 15 dc in ring. Join with sl st in top of ch 3. 16 dc.

2nd rnd: *Ch 3. 3 dc in same sp as last sl st. Drop loop from hook. Insert hook in top of ch 3 and draw dropped loop through. Ch 1 to close st* – beg popcorn made. *2 dc in each of next 2 dc. *4 dc in next dc. Drop loop from hook. Insert hook in first of 4 dc and draw dropped loop through. Ch 1 to close st* – popcorn made. Ch 5. Popcorn in next dc. Rep from * to last 3 dc. 2 dc in each of next 2 dc. Popcorn in last dc. Ch 5. Join with sl st to top of beg popcorn.

3rd rnd: Sl st in next dc. Beg popcorn in same sp as sl st. 1 dc in each of next 2 dc. Popcorn in next dc. *Break A. Join B. Ch 2. 5 dc in next ch-5 sp. Ch 2.** Break B. Join A. Miss next popcorn. Popcorn in next dc. 1 dc in each of next 2 dc. Popcorn in next dc. Rep from * twice more, then rep from * to ** once. Join with sl st to top of beg popcorn. Fasten off.

4th rnd: Join A with sl st to next dc. Beg popcorn in same sp as sl st. Popcorn in next dc. *Break A. Join B. Ch 2. 1 dc in next ch-2 sp. 1 dc in next dc. 2 dc in next dc. 3 dc in next dc. 2 dc in next dc. 1 dc in next dc. 1 dc in next ch-2 sp. Ch 2.** Break B. Join A. Miss next popcorn. (Popcorn in next dc) twice. Rep from * twice more, then rep from * to ** once. Join with sl st to top of beg popcorn. Fasten off.

5th rnd: Join A with sl st to top of first beg popcorn. *Ch 3. 1 dc in same sp as last sl st. 2 dc in top of next 4 dc. Drop loop from hook. Insert hook in top of ch 3 and draw dropped loop through. Ch 1 to close st* – beg popcorn 2tog made. *Break A. Join B. Ch 2. 1 dc in next ch-2 sp. 1 dc in each of next 4 dc. 2 dc in next dc. 3 dc in next dc. 2 dc in next dc. 1 dc in each of next 4 dc. 1 dc in next ch-2 sp. Ch 2.** Break B. Join A. *(2 dc in top of next popcorn) twice. Drop loop from hook. Insert hook in first dc and draw dropped loop through. Ch 1 to close st* – popcorn 2tog made. Rep from * twice more, then rep from * to ** once. Join B with sl st to top of beg popcorn 2tog.

6th rnd: With B, ch 3. *2 dc in next ch-2 sp. 1 dc in each of next 8 dc. (2 dc. Ch 2. 2 dc) in next dc. 1 dc in each of next 8 dc. 2 dc in next ch-2 sp.** 1 dc in top of popcorn 2tog. Rep from * twice more, then rep from * to ** once. Break B. Join C with sl st to top of ch 3.

7th rnd: With C, ch 2 (does not count as st). 1 hdc in same sp as last sl st. (Dcbp around post of next dc. 1 hdc in next dc) 6 times. *(2 hdc. Ch 2. 2 hdc) in next ch-2 sp. (1 hdc in next dc. Dcbp around post of next dc) 12 times. 1 hdc in next dc. Rep from * twice more. (2 hdc. Ch 2. 2 hdc) in next ch-2 sp. (1 hdc in next dc. Dcbp around post of next dc) 6 times. Join with sl st to first hdc.

Note: Carry color when not in use in next rnd loosely across top of previous rnd and work sts around it to avoid stranding.

8th rnd: With C, ch 2 (does not count as hdc). 1 hdc in same sp as last sl st. (Join D. With D, 1 hdc in each of next 2 sts. Join C. With C, 1 hdc in each of next 2 sts) 3 times. Join D. With D, 1 hdc in each of next 2 sts. *Join C. With C, (2 hdc. Ch 2. 2 hdc) in next ch-2 sp. Join D. With D, 1 hdc in next st. (Join C. With C, 1 hdc in each of next 2 sts. Join D. With D, 1 hdc in each of next 2 sts) 7 times. Rep from * twice more. Join C. With C, (2 hdc. Ch 2. 2 hdc) in next ch-2 sp. Join D. With D, 1 hdc in next st. (Join C. With C, 1 hdc in each of next 2 sts. Join D. With D, 1 hdc in each of next 2 sts) 3 times. Join C. With C, 1 hdc in last st. Join E with sl st to first hdc. Break C and D.

9th rnd: With E, ch 1. 1 sc in same sp as last sl st. 1 sc in each of next 16 hdc. *(1 sc. Ch 2. 1 sc) in next ch-2 sp. 1 sc in each of next 33 hdc. Rep from * twice more. (1 sc. Ch 2. 1 sc) in next ch-2 sp. 1 sc in each of last 16 hdc. Join A with sl st to first sc. Break E.

10th rnd: With A, ch 1. 1 sc in same sp as last sl st. 1 sc in each of next 17 sc. *(1 sc. Ch 2. 1 sc) in next ch-2 sp. 1 sc in each of next 35 sc. Rep from * twice more. (1 sc. Ch 2. 1 sc) in next ch-2 sp. 1 sc in each of last 17 sc. Join with sl st to first sc. Fasten off.

11th rnd: Join B with sl st from back to front around post of same sc as last sl st. Ch 3. Dcbp around post of next 18 sc. *(2 hdc. Ch 2. 2 hdc) in next ch-2 sp. Dcbp around post of next 37 sc. Rep from * twice more. (2 hdc. Ch 2. 2 hdc) in next ch-2 sp. Dcbp around post of next 18 sc. Join C with sl st in top of ch 3. Break B.

12th rnd: With C, ch 2 (does not count as st). 1 hdc in same sp as last sl st. (Dcbp around post of next st. 1 hdc in next st) 10 times. *(2 hdc. Ch 2. 2 hdc) in next ch-2 sp. (1 hdc in next st. Dcbp around post of next st) 20 times. 1 hdc in next st. Rep from * twice more. (1 hdc. Ch 2. 1 hdc) in next ch-2 sp. (1 hdc in next st. Dcbp around post of next st) 10 times. Join D with sl st to first hdc. Break C.

Note: Carry color when not in use in 13th and 14th rnds loosely across top of previous rnd and work sts around it to avoid stranding.

13th rnd: With D, ch 3. 1 dc in next st. (Join E. With E, 1 dc in each of next 3 sts. Join D. With D, 1 dc in each of next 3 sts) 3 times. Join E. With E, 1 dc in each of next 3 sts. *Join D. With D, (2 dc. Ch 2. 2 dc) in next ch-2 sp. ** (Join E. With E, 1 dc in each of next 3 sts. Join D. With D, 1 dc in each of next 3 sts) 7 times. Join E. With E, 1 dc in each of next 3 sts. Rep from * twice more, then rep from * to ** once. (Join E. With E, 1 dc in each of next 3 sts. Join D. With D, 1 dc in each of next 3 sts) 3 times. Join E. With E, 1 dc in each of next 3 sts. Join D. With D, 1 dc in last st. Join with sl st in top of ch 3.

14th rnd: With D, ch 3. 1 dc in next st. (Join E. With E, 1 dc in each of next 3 sts. Join D. With D, 1 dc in each of next 3 sts) 3 times. Join E. With E, 1 dc in each of next 5 sts. *Join D. With D, (2 dc. Ch 2. 2 dc) in next ch-2 sp. Join E. With E, 1 dc in each of next 5 sts.** (Join D. With D, 1 dc in each of next 3 sts. Join E. With E, 1 dc in each of next 3 sts) 7 times. With E, 1 dc in each of next 2 sts. Rep from * twice more, then rep from * to ** once. (Join D. With D, 1 dc in each of next 3 sts. Join E. With E, 1 dc in each of next 3 sts) 3 times. Join D. With D, 1 dc in last st. Join with sl st in top of ch 3. Join with sl st in top of ch 3. Fasten off.

FINISHING

Join Motifs: Join all sides of Base Motif to other 2 Side Motifs.

(See Assembly Diagram on page 9)

To join sides: Place RS of Motifs facing each other, having Base Motif on top of work and pin sides in position. *Working through both thicknesses,* join D with sl st in any corner ch-2 sp. Ch 1. (Work 1 row of sc to next corner ch-2 sp. 3 sc in corner) 4 times. Join with sl st to first sc. Fasten off.

With WS of work facing, steam press lightly along seams to flatten.

Back Inset

(See Chart II on page 11).

Note: Ch 3 at beg of row counts as dc throughout.

**With A, ch 4.

1st row: (RS). 2 dc in 4th ch from hook (counts as 3 dc). Turn.

2nd row: Ch 3. 1 dc in first dc. 1 dc in next dc. 2 dc in top of turning ch. Turn. 5 dc.

3rd row: Ch 3. 1 dc in first dc. 1 dc in each dc to turning ch. 2 dc in top of turning ch.

4th to 6th rows: As 3rd row. 13 dc at end of 6th row.**

Place markers at each end of last row.

7th to 13th rows: Ch 3. 1 dc in each dc to end of row, ending with 1 dc in top of turning ch. Turn.

14th row: Ch 3. 1 dc in each of next 5 dc. Ch 1. Miss next dc for toggle hole. 1 dc in each of next 5 dc. 1 dc in top of turning ch. Turn.

15th row: Ch 3. 1 dc in each of next 5 dc. 1 dc in next ch-1 sp. 1 dc in each of next 5 dc. 1 dc in top of turning ch. Turn.

16th row: Ch 3. Dc2tog. 1 dc in each st to last 3 sts. Dc2tog. 1 dc in top of turning ch. Turn.

17th row: As 16th row. 9 sts. Fasten off.

Front Inset

Work from ** to ** as given for Back Inset.

7th row: Ch 3. 1 dc in each dc to end of row, ending with 1 dc in top of turning ch. Fasten off.

Sew sides of Front Inset in position as shown in picture. Sew sides of Back Inset to markers into same position on opposite side of Bag. Sew toggle in position to Front Inset.

Strap: Place markers on top corners of 2 Side Motifs on 5th dc on each side of ch-2 sp.

First Half: 1st row: (RS). Join A with sl st in first marker of either Side Motif. Ch 3. 1 dc in next dc. 1 hdc in each of next 2 dc. 1 sc in next dc. 1 sc in next ch-2 sp. 1 sc in next dc. 1 hdc in each of next 2 dc. 1 dc in each of next 2 dc. Turn. 11 sts.

2nd row: Ch 2 (does not count as st). Hdc2tog. 1 hdc in each of next 7 sts. Hdc2tog. Turn. 9 sts.

3rd row: Ch 2 (does not count as st). 1 hdc in each st to end of row. Turn.

Rep last row until Strap measures 11" [28 cm] when slightly stretched. Fasten off.

Second Half: Work as for First Half in marked corner of rem Side Motif. **Do not** fasten off.

Join Halves: Place RS of Halves tog with Second Half on top of work. *Working through both thicknesses,* ch 1. Work 1 row of sc to end of row. Fasten off. BERNAT

Assembly Diagram

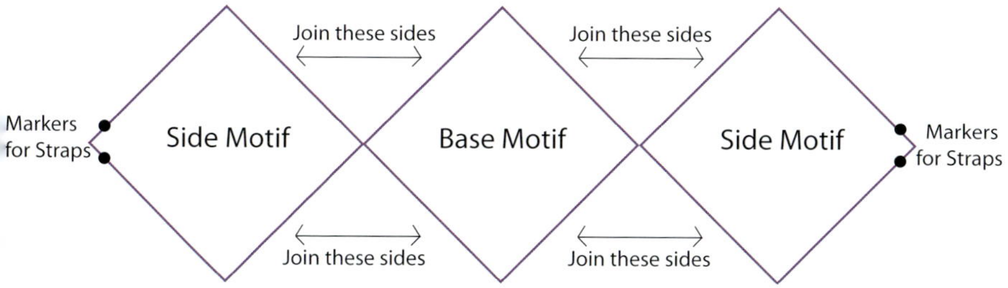

Chart I

Chart II

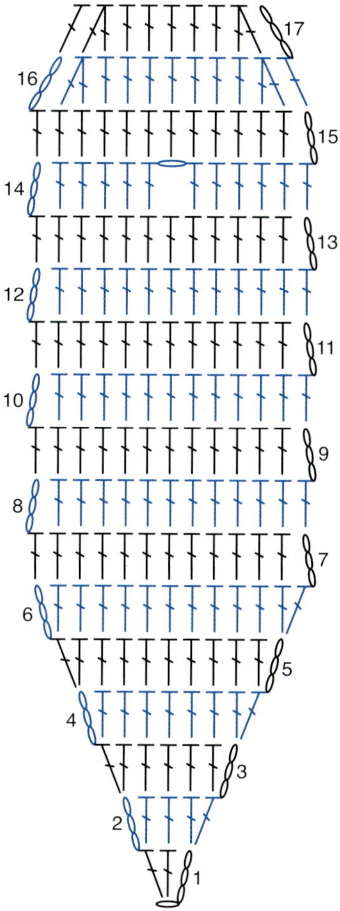
17
16
15
14
13
12
11
10
9
8
7
6
5
4
3
2
1

Key

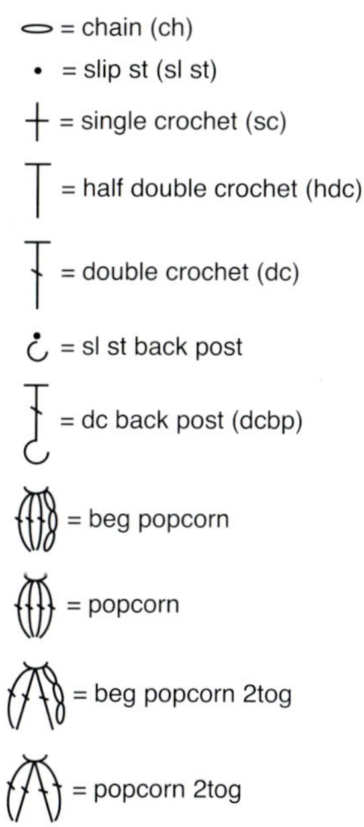
= chain (ch)
= slip st (sl st)
= single crochet (sc)
= half double crochet (hdc)
= double crochet (dc)
= sl st back post
= dc back post (dcbp)
= beg popcorn
= popcorn
= beg popcorn 2tog
= popcorn 2tog

2. Nautical Hobo Bag (crochet)

4 MEDIUM

EASY

MEASUREMENTS

Approx 46" [117 cm] around, at widest point x 18" [45.5 cm] high, excluding handles.

GAUGE

15 sc and 16 rows = 4" [10 cm] with smaller hook.

ABBREVIATIONS

See page 41 for Helpful Hints

Approx = Approximately

Beg = Beginning

Ch = Chain(s)

Cont = Continue(ity)

Hdc = Half double crochet

Hdc2tog = (Yoh and draw up a loop in next stitch) twice. Yoh and draw through all loops on hook.

Inc = Increase(ing)

Rep = Repeat(ing)

Rnd(s) = Round(s)

Sc = Single crochet

Sl st = Slip stitch

Sp(s) = Space(s)

St(s) = Stitch(es)

Tog = Together

Yoh = Yarn over hook

MATERIALS

Bernat® Handicrafter® Cotton (50 g/1.75 oz; 73 m/80 yds)		
Contrast A Indigo (13114)	**8 balls**	**535 m/585 yds**
Contrast B Off White (00002)	**10 balls**	**670 m/737 yds**
Contrast C French Blue (00010)	**2 balls**	**140 m/153 yds**

Sizes 3.75 mm (U.S. F/ 5) and 5 mm (U.S. H/8) crochet hooks **or size needed to obtain gauge.** 8 large grommets ¾" [2 cm]. 2 separating rings 3" [7.5 cm] diameter.

INSTRUCTIONS

Notes: When joining colors, work to last 2 loops on hook of first color. Draw new color through last 2 loops and proceed.

Ch 2 at beg of rnd does not count as st. Join with sl st to first st at end of each rnd.

With A, and smaller hook, ch 4. Join with sl st to first ch to form a ring.

1st rnd: Ch 2. 8 hdc in ring. Join with sl st to first hdc.

2nd rnd: Ch 2. 2 hdc in each hdc around. Join with sl st to first hdc. 16 hdc.

3rd rnd: Ch 2. (2 hdc in next hdc. 1 hdc in next hdc) 8 times. Join with sl st to first hdc. 24 hdc.

4th rnd: Ch 2. (2 hdc in next hdc. 1 hdc in each of next 2 hdc) 8 times. Join with sl st to first hdc. 32 hdc.

5th rnd: Ch 2. (2 hdc in next hdc. 1 hdc in each of next 3 hdc) 8 times. Join with sl st to first hdc. 40 hdc.

6th rnd: Ch 2. (2 hdc in next hdc. 1 hdc in each of next 4 hdc) 8 times. Join with sl st to first hdc. 48 hdc.
Cont as established, inc 8 hdc every rnd until there are 184 hdc.
Join B at end of last rnd.

Proceed as follows:
1st to 14th rnds: With B, ch 2. 1 hdc in sp between each hdc around. Join with sl st to first hdc.
With C, rep last rnd once more. Join B.
With B, rep last rnd 3 times more. Join A.
With A, rep last rnd 9 times more. Join B.
With B, rep last rnd 5 times more.
Next rnd: With B, ch 2. (Hdc2tog. 1 hdc in sp between each of next 21 hdc) 8 times. 176 sts.
Next 3 rnds: Ch 2. 1 hdc in sp between each st around. Join with sl st to first hdc.
Next rnd: Ch 2. (Hdc2tog. 1 hdc in sp between each of next 20 hdc) 8 times. 168 sts.
Next 3 rnds: Ch 2. 1 hdc in sp between each st around. Join with sl st to first hdc.
Next rnd: Ch 2. (Hdc2tog. 1 hdc in sp between each of next 19 hdc) 8 times. 160 sts.
Next 8 rnds: Ch 2. 1 hdc in sp between each st around. Join C with sl st to first hdc at end of last rnd.
With C, rep last rnd twice more. Fasten off.

FINISHING

Fold top 4" [10 cm] down to RS and sew in position.

To mark placement for grommets:
(See Diagram on page 15).
Lay Bag flat. Mark centers at front and back of Bag.
Place 4 markers 7" [18 cm] and 10" [25.5 cm] on each side of center on front and back. (8 markers total).

Apply grommets 1½" [4 cm] down from top of Bag following manufacturer's instructions.

Fold in edges of Bag, lining up 4 grommets (see photo). Insert metal ring through 4 grommets. Rep on other side of Bag.

With larger hook, join A with sl st to ring. Ch 1. Work 1 rnd of sc around diameter of ring. Join with sl st to first sc. Rep for other ring.

Strap
First Half: 1st row: (RS). With larger crochet hook, join 2 strands of A with sl st to any sc at top of Ring. Ch 1. 1 sc in each of next 8 sc. Turn.
2nd row: Ch 1. 1 sc in each sc to end of row. Turn.
Rep last row until Strap measures 10" [25.5 cm] when slightly stretched. Fasten off.

Second Half: Work as for First Half in other Ring. **Do not** fasten off.

Join Halves: Place RS of Halves tog with Second Half on top of work. *Working through both thicknesses,* ch 1. Work 1 row of sc to end of row. Fasten off.

Place markers 1½" [4 cm] up from each Ring along side of Strap.

Fold Strap in half lengthwise and *working through both thicknesses*, work 1 row of sc between markers to join sides tog. Fasten off. BERNAT

DIAGRAM FOR GROMMET PLACEMENT

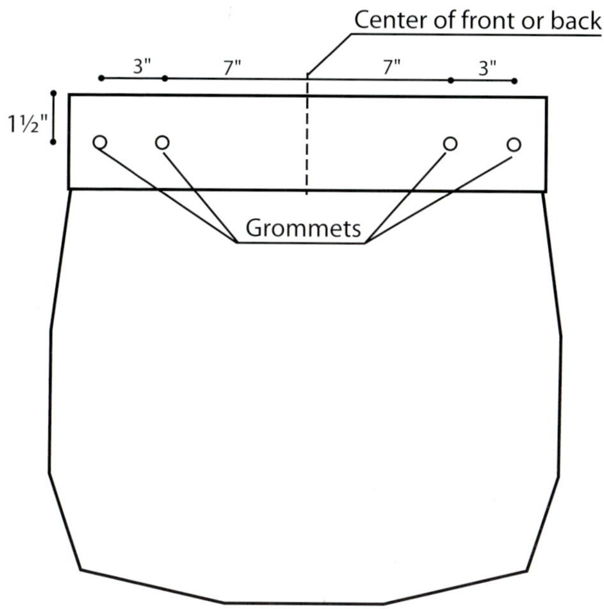

3. Orange Slice Purse (crochet)

4 MEDIUM

INTERMEDIATE

MEASUREMENTS

Approx 13" [33 cm] wide x 10" [25.5 cm] high (excluding handle).

GAUGE

16 sc and 17 rows = 4" [10 cm].

ABBREVIATIONS

See page 41 for Helpful Hints

Alt = Alternate(ing)
Approx = Approximately
Beg = Beginning
Ch = Chain(s)
Dc = Double crochet
Dcbp = Yoh and draw up a loop around post of next stitch at back of work, inserting hook from right to left. (Yoh and draw through 2 loops on hook) twice.
Dec = Decrease(ing)
Inc = Increase(ing)
Rem = Remaining
Rep = Repeat
RS = Right side
Sc = Single crochet
Sl st = Slip stitch
Sts = Stitch(es)
Tog = Together
WS = Wrong side
Yoh = Yarn over hook

MATERIALS

Bernat® Handicrafter® Cotton (50 g/1.75 oz; 73 m/80 yds)		
 Tangerine (13699)	**4 balls**	**250 m/275 yds**
Size 3.75 mm (U.S. F/5) crochet hook **or size needed to obtain gauge.** Purchased handle approx 22" [56 cm] long with metal rings.		

INSTRUCTIONS

Front and Back (make 2 pieces alike).
(See Chart III on page 19).
Ch 27.

1st row: (RS). *Working in horizontal 'bump' at back of each ch,* sl st in 2nd ch from hook. Sl st in each ch to end of chain. Turn. 26 sts.

2nd row: Ch 1. *Working in back loops only,* sl st in each of next 22 sts. **Turn.** Leave rem sts unworked.

3rd and alt rows: Ch 1. *Working in back loops only,* sl st in each st to end of row. Turn.

4th row: Ch 1. *Working in back loops only,* sl st in each of next 18 sts. **Turn.** Leave rem sts unworked.

6th row: Ch 1. *Working in back loops only,* sl st in each of next 14 sts. **Turn.** Leave rem sts unworked.

8th row: Ch 1. *Working in back loops only,* sl st in each of next 10 sts. **Turn.** Leave rem sts unworked.

10th row: Ch 1. *Working in back loops only,* sl st in each of next 10 sts. Sl st in each of next 4 missed sts. **Turn.** Leave rem sts unworked.

12th row: Ch 1. *Working in back loops only,* sl st in each of next 14 sts. Sl st in each of next 4 missed sts. **Turn.** Leave rem sts unworked.

14th row: Ch 1. *Working in back loops only,* sl st in each of next 18 sts. Sl st in each of next 4 missed sts. **Turn.** Leave rem sts unworked.

16th row: Ch 1. *Working in back loops only,* sl st in each of next 22 sts. Sl st in each of next 4 missed sts. Turn. 26 sts.

17th row: As 3rd row.

Rep 2nd to 17th rows 7 times more, then rep 2nd to 16th rows once. Fasten off, leaving a long end. Thread end onto tapestry needle and draw tightly through narrow row ends at center. Fasten securely.

Edging: (See Chart IV on page 19).

1st row: (RS). Join yarn with sl st at outer edge. Ch 1. Work 73 sc along outer edge to opposite corner. Fasten off.

2nd row: (RS). *Inserting hook from back to front,* work sl st around post of 1st sc of last row. Ch 2 (counts as st). Dcbp around post of each sc to end of row. Fasten off.

Join Front and Back: Place RS of Front and Back tog and pin edging sts tog. *Working through both thicknesses and in back loop only of each st across,* join yarn with sl st in first dcbp. Sl st in each dcbp to end of row. Fasten off.

Sew handle rings in position at each side of Bag as shown in picture. BERNAT

CHART III

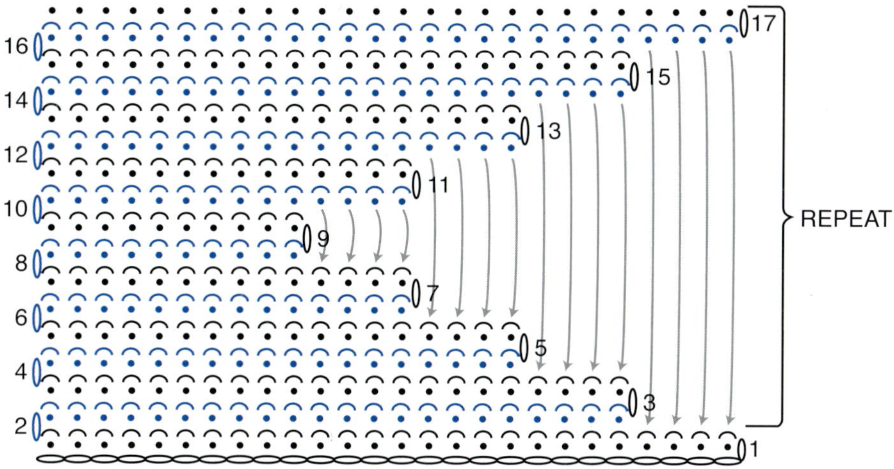

CHART IV

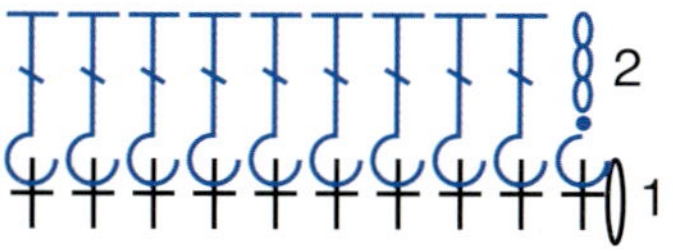

KEY

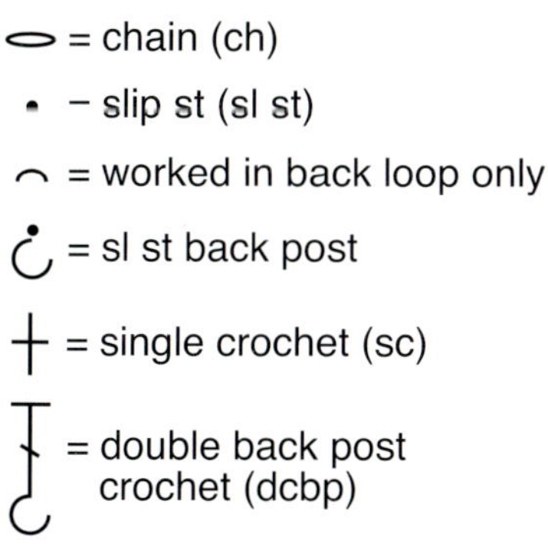

4. Graphic Motif Bag (crochet)

4 MEDIUM

INTERMEDIATE

MEASUREMENTS

Approx 10" [25.5 cm] wide x 11" [28 cm] high, excluding handles.

GAUGE

13 sc and 14 rows = 4" [10 cm].

ABBREVIATIONS

See page 41 for Helpful Hints

Approx = Approximately
Beg = Beginning
Ch = Chain(s)
Dc = Double crochet
Rep = Repeat(ing)
Rem = Remain(ing)
Rnd(s) = Round(s)
RS = Right side
Sc = Single crochet
Sc2tog = Draw up a loop in each of next 2 stitches. Yoh and draw through all loops on hook.
Sl st = Slip stitch
Sp(s) = Space(s)
St(s) = Stitch(es)
Tog = Together
WS = Wrong side
Yoh = Yarn over hook

MATERIALS

Bernat® Handicrafter® Cotton (50 g/1.75 oz; 73 m/80 yds)		
 **Main Color (MC)** Off White (00002)	**2 balls**	**115 m/126 yds**
 **Contrast A** Black Liquorice (13040)	**2 balls**	**100 m/110 yds**
Size 5 mm (U.S. H/8) crochet hook **or size needed to obtain gauge.** ¼ yds [0.25 m] of fabric for lining. Pair of purchased handles.		

INSTRUCTIONS

Note: Bag has 5 motifs joined tog.

First Motif

(See Chart V on page 24).

With MC, ch 10. Join with sl st to first ch to form ring.

1st rnd: Ch 3 (counts as dc). 23 dc in ring. Join with sl st to top of ch 3. 24 dc.

2nd rnd: Ch 1. 1 sc in each of first 3 dc. *(1 sc. Ch 7. 1 sc) in next dc.** 1 sc in each of next 5 dc. Rep from * twice more, then from * to ** once. 1 sc in each of last 2 sc. Join with sl st to first sc.

3rd rnd: Ch 1. (1 sc. Ch 7. 1 sc) in first sc. *Miss next 2 sc. (7 dc. *Ch 3. Sl st in first ch* – picot made. 6 dc) all in next ch-7 sp. Miss next 2 sc.** (1 sc. Ch 7. 1 sc) all in next sc. Rep from * twice more, then from * to ** once. Join with sl st to first sc. Fasten off.

To join 2 Motifs: Work 1st and 2nd rnds as given for First Motif.

3rd rnd: Ch 1. (1 sc. Ch 7. 1 sc) in first sc. *Miss next 2 sc. (7 dc. Ch 3. Picot. 6 dc) all in next ch-7 sp. Miss next 2 sc. (1 sc. Ch 7. 1 sc) all in next sc. Rep from * once more. **Miss next 2 sc. (7 dc. Ch 2. Sl st in corresponding picot of adjoining Motif. Ch 1. Sl st in first ch. 6 dc) all in next ch-7 sp. Miss next 2 sc.** (1 sc. Ch 3. 1 sc in 4th ch of next ch-7 sp of adjoining Motif. Ch 3. 1 sc) in next sc. Rep from ** to **. Join with sl st to first sc. Fasten off.

Join 4 Motifs to form strip.

Fifth Motif: To join last Motif to previous and first Motifs: Work 1st and 2nd rnds as given for First Motif.

3rd rnd: Ch 1. (1 sc. Ch 7. 1 sc) in first sc. *Miss next 2 sc. (7 dc. Ch 2. Sl st in corresponding picot of First Motif. Ch 1. Sl st in first ch. 6 dc) all in next ch-7 sp. Miss next 2 sc.** (1 sc. Ch 3. 1 sc in 4th ch of next ch 7 of First Motif. Ch 3. 1 sc) in next sc. Rep from * to ** once more. (1 sc. Ch 7. 1 sc) in next sc. Miss next 2 sc. (7 dc. Ch 2. Sl st in corresponding picot of First Motif. Ch 1. Sl st in first ch. 6 dc) all in next ch-7 sp. Miss next 2 sc. (1 sc. Ch 3. 1 sc in 4th ch of next ch 7 of First Motif. Ch 3. 1 sc) in next sc. Miss next 2 sc. (7 dc. Ch 2. Sl st in corresponding picot of First Motif. Ch 1. Sl st in first ch. 6 dc) all in next ch-7 sp. Miss next 2 sc. Join with sl st to first sc. Fasten off.

Edging

1st rnd: ***Join MC with sl st to any ch-7 sp. Ch 1. 1 sc in same sp as sl st. *Ch 3. Miss next 3 dc. 1 sc in next dc. Ch 3. 1 sc in next picot. Ch 3. Miss next 3 dc. 1 sc in next dc. Ch 3. 1 sc in next ch-7 sp. Rep from * around. Join with sl st to first sc.

2nd rnd: Ch 1. Work 3 sc in each ch-3 sp and 1 sc in each sc around. Join A with sl st to first sc. Break MC. 80 sc.

3rd rnd: With A, ch 1. 1 sc in each sc around. Join with sl st to first sc.

4th rnd: Ch 1. *1 sc in each of next 6 sc. Sc2tog. Rep from * around. Join with sl st to first sc. 70 sts.

5th rnd: Ch 1. 1 sc in each st around. Join with sl st to first sc.

6th rnd: Ch 1. *1 sc in each of next 5 sc. Sc2tog. Rep from * around. Join with sl st to first sc. 60 sts.***

Beg working in rows:

First side: 1st row: Ch 1. 1 sc in each of next 30 sts. **Turn.** Leave rem sts unworked.

******2nd row:** Ch 1. 1 sc in each sc to end of row. Turn. Place marker at end of row.

3rd row: Ch 1. (Sc2tog. 1 sc in each of next 12 sc) twice. Sc2tog. Turn. 27 sts.

4th row: Ch 1. 1 sc in each st to end of row. Turn.

Rep last row until work from marked row measures 2" [5 cm]. Fasten off.****

Second side: 1st row: With RS facing, join A with sl st to first rem st. Ch 1. 1 sc in same sp as sl st and each of next 29 sc. Turn.

Work from **** to **** as given for First side.

Base

Work from *** to *** as given for Edging. Fasten off. Lay Bag flat, sew bottom edge closed.

With WS facing, fold 2 bottom corners of Bag flat. Using backstitch, sew straight across 1½" [4 cm] down from top corner to form bottom of Bag.

FINISHING

Fold top edge through handles and sew into position to marked row.

Lining: Cut lining fabric 7½" [19 cm] x 11" [28 cm]. Fold fabric in half with RS tog and sew side seams having ½" [1 cm] seam allowance.

Fold top edge of lining down 1" [2.5 cm] at top edge and press.

With WS tog, insert Lining in Bag and tack into place at bottom corners.

Using whip stitch, sew top edge of Lining to inside of Bag to first marked row. BERNAT

Crochet Hook Conversion Chart

Canadian & U.K. Sizes	000	00	0	2	3	4	5	6	7	8	-	9	10	11	-	12	13	14
Metric Sizes (mm)	10	9	8	7	6.50	6	5.50	5	4.50	4	3.75	3.5	3.25	3	2.75	2.5	2.25	2
U.S. Sizes	N 15	M 13	L 11	-	K 10½	J 10	I 9	H 8	7	G 6	F 5	E 4	D 3	-	C 2	-	B 1	-

CHART V

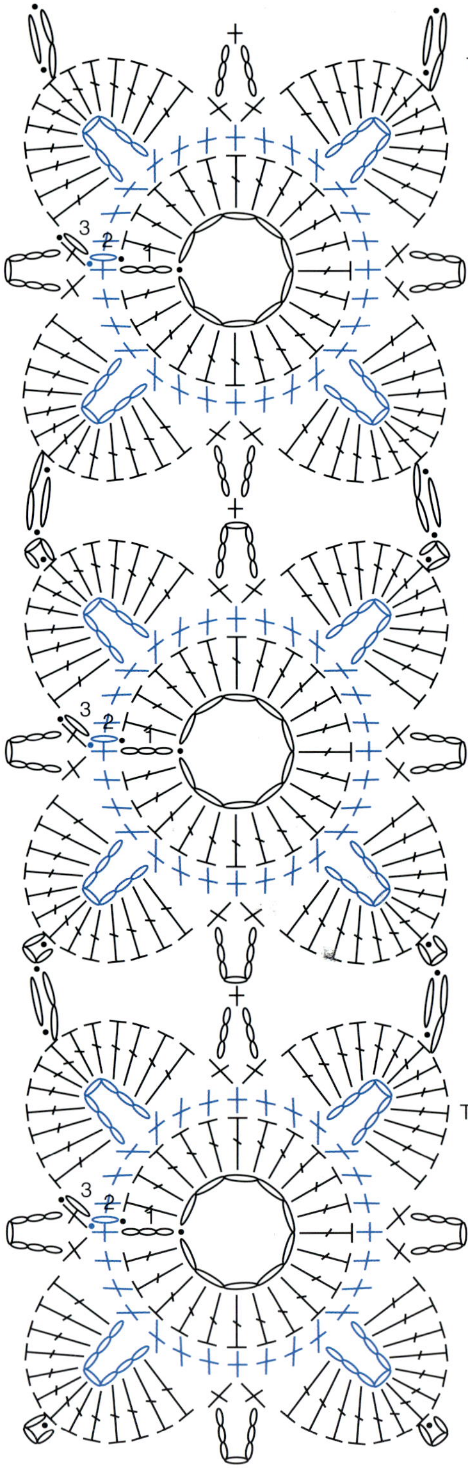

KEY

= chain (ch)

= slip st (sl st)

= single crochet (sc)

= double crochet (dc)

= picot

5. Easy, Breezy Carry-All (crochet)

MEDIUM

EASY

MEASUREMENT

Approx 25" [63.5 cm] high, excluding handles.

GAUGE

13 sc and 14 rows = 4" [10 cm].

ABBREVIATIONS

See page 41 for Helpful Hints

Approx = Approximately
Beg = Beginning
Ch = Chain(s)
Pat = Pattern
Rep = Repeat(s)
RS = Right side
Sc = Single crochet
Sl st = Slip stitch
Sp(s) = Space(s)
Tr = Treble crochet
WS = Wrong side

MATERIALS

Bernat® Handicrafter® Cotton (50 g/1.75 oz; 73 m/80 yds)		
 **Contrast A** Indigo (13114)	**6 balls**	**421 m/463 yds**
 **Contrast B** French Blue (00010)	**2 balls**	**100 m/110 yds**
 **Contrast C** Tangerine (13699)	**2 balls**	**80 m/88 yds**
Size 5 mm (U.S. H/8) crochet hook **or size needed to obtain gauge.**		

INSTRUCTIONS

Stripe Pat: Work 2 rows of each color in the following sequence: B, A, C, A, B, A. These 12 rows form Stripe Pat.

Body: With A, ch 55.

1st row: (RS). 1 sc in 2nd ch from hook. 1 sc in each ch to end of ch. Turn. 54 sc.

2nd to 4th rows: Ch 1. 1 sc in each sc to end of row. Turn.

Proceed in Stripe Pat as follows:

1st row: (RS). With A, ch 6 (counts as tr and ch 2). *1 tr in next sc. Ch 2. Rep from * to last sc. 1 tr in last sc. Turn.

2nd row: Ch 6 (counts as tr and ch 2). *Miss next ch-2 sp. 1 tr in next tr. Ch 2. Rep from * to last ch 6. 1 tr in 4th ch of ch 6. Turn.

First 2 rows of Stripe Pat are complete.

Rep 2nd row until work from beg measures 25" [63.5 cm], ending with a WS row.

Next row: With A, ch 1. 1 sc in first tr. *Miss next ch-2 sp. 1 sc in next tr. Rep from * to end of row. Turn.
Next 3 rows: Ch 1. 1 sc in each sc to end of row. Turn. Fasten off at end of last row.

Handles: With RS of work facing join A with sl st to top left corner of Bag. Ch 1. Work 38 sc evenly across side of Bag. Turn.

Next row: Ch 57 (handle). 1 sc in 2nd ch from hook. 1 sc in each of next 55 ch. 1 sc in each sc to end of row. Turn. 94 sc in total.

Next 2 rows: Ch 1. 1 sc in each sc to end of row. Turn. Fasten off at end of last row, leaving a long end.

Sew end of Handle in position. Rep for other side. (See Diagram). BERNAT

DIAGRAM

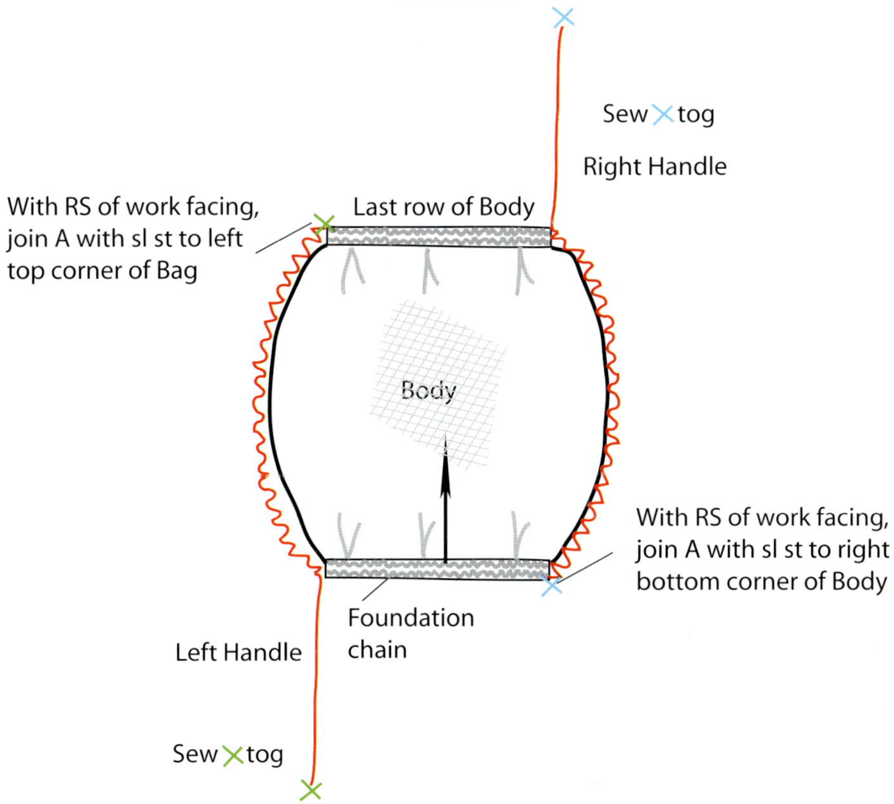

6. On the Side Tote (crochet)

4 MEDIUM

INTERMEDIATE

MEASUREMENTS

Approx 16" x 17" [40.5 x 43 cm].

GAUGE

13 sc and 14 rows = 4" [10 cm].

ABBREVIATIONS

See page 41 for Helpful Hints.

Approx = Approximately
Beg = Beginning
Ch = Chain(s)
Cont = Continue(ity)
Dc = Double crochet
Pat = Pattern
Rem = Remaining
Rep = Repeat(s)
RS = Right side
Sc = Single crochet
Sc2tog = Draw up a loop in each of next 2 stitches. Yoh and draw through all loops on hook.
Sl st = Slip stitch
St(s) = Stitch(es)
Sp(s) = Space(s)
WS = Wrong side
Yoh = Yarn over hook

MATERIALS

Bernat® Handicrafter® Cotton (50 g/1.75 oz; 73 m/80 yds)		
Contrast A Hot Blue (13742)	**3 balls**	**215 m/235 yds**
Contrast B Hot Orange (13628)	**3 balls**	**200 m/220 yds**
Contrast C Hot Green (13712)	**3 balls**	**210 m/230 yds**
Size 5 mm (U.S. H/8) crochet hook **or size needed to obtain gauge.**		

INSTRUCTIONS

Stripe Pat: Work 1 row of each color: A, B, C. These 3 rows form Stripe Pat.

Note: Do not break color at end of row. Carry color not in use loosely up side of work.

First Section: (See Diagram on page 32) With A, ch 26.

1st row: (RS). 1 sc in 2nd ch from hook. *Ch 1. Miss next ch. 1 sc in next ch. Rep from * to end of chain. Join B. Turn. 25 sts.

2nd row: With B, *ch 2. 1 dc in next ch-1 sp* - counts as beg dc2tog. **Yoh and draw up a loop in same ch-1 sp as last st. Yoh and draw through 2 loops on hook. Yoh and draw up a loop in next ch-1 sp. Yoh and draw through 2 loops on hook. Yoh and draw through all 3 loops on hook* - dc2tog made. Ch 1. Rep from * to last sc. Dc2tog over last worked ch-1 sp and last sc. Join C. Turn.

3rd row: With C, ch 1. 1 sc in first st. *1 sc in next ch-1 sp. Ch 1. Miss next st. Rep from * to last ch-1 sp. 1 sc in last ch-1 sp. 1 sc in last st. Join A. Turn.

4th row: With A, ch 3 (counts as dc). Dc2tog over first st and next ch-1 sp. *Ch 1. Miss next sc. Dc2tog over last worked ch-1 sp and next ch-1 sp. Rep from * to last sc. Dc2tog over last worked ch-1 sp and last sc. 1 dc in last sc. Join B. Turn.

5th row: With B, ch 1. 1 sc in first st. *Ch 1. Miss next st. 1 sc in next ch-1 sp. Rep from * to last 2 sts. Ch 1. Miss next st. 1 sc in last st. Join C. Turn.

2nd to 5th rows form Zig-Zag pat.

Keeping cont of Stripe Pat, rep last 4 rows until work from beg measures approx 6" [15 cm], ending on a 5th row. Fasten off.

Second Section: 1st row: (WS). With appropriate color, ch 25. With WS facing, pat across 25 sts of First Section. Ch 26. Join next color. Turn.

2nd row: 1 sc in 2nd ch from hook. *1 sc in next ch-1 sp. Ch 1. Miss next ch. Rep from * to last ch. 1 sc in last ch. **Ch 1. Miss next st. 1 sc in next ch-1 sp. Rep from ** to last st of First Section. Ch 1. Miss last st. ***1 sc in next ch. Ch 1. Miss next ch. Rep from *** to last ch. 1 sc in last ch. Join next color. Turn. 75 sts.

Beg with 4th row of Zig-Zag pat, work for next 6" [15 cm], ending on a 5th row.

Third Section: 1st row: (WS). Pat across 75 sts of Second Section. Ch 51. Join next color. Turn.

2nd row: 1 sc in 2nd ch from hook. *1 sc in next ch-1 sp. Ch 1. Miss next ch. Rep from * to last ch. 1 sc in last ch. **Ch 1. Miss next st. 1 sc in next ch-1 sp. Rep from ** to last ch-1 sp. 1 sc in last ch-1 sp. 1 sc in last st. Join next color. Turn.

Beg with 4th row of Zig-Zag pat, work for next 6" [15 cm], ending on a 4th row.

Fourth Section: 1st row: (RS). Ch 1. 1 sc in first st. (Ch 1. Miss next st. 1 sc in next ch-1 sp) 36 times. Ch 1. Miss next st. 1 sc in last st. **Turn.** Leave rem sts unworked.

Beg with 2nd row of Zig-Zag pat, work for next 6" [15 cm], ending on a 4th row. Fasten off.

Fifth Section: 1st row: (RS). Miss first 25 sts (ch-1 sps and dc2tog). Join appropriate color in next dc2tog. Ch 1. 1 sc in same sp as sl st. (1 sc in next ch-1 sp. Ch 1. Miss next st) 11 times. 1 sc in next ch-1 sp. 1 sc in next st. **Turn.** Leave rem sts unworked.

Beg with 2nd row of Zig-Zag pat, work for next 6" [15 cm], ending on a 4th row. Fasten off.

Sew corresponding sides. (See Assembly Diagram on page 32).

Opening edging: 1st rnd: With RS facing, join A with sl st to any outer corner. Ch 1. Work 18 sc along each side, having 3 sc in outer corners and sc2tog in inner corners. Join with sl st to first sc.

2nd rnd: As 1st rnd. Fasten off.

Straps: (Make 2).

With A, ch 80.

1st rnd: 1 dc in 4th ch from hook. 1 dc in each ch to end of ch. *Working into rem loops along opposite side of ch*, work 1 dc in each ch to end of ch. Ch 1. **Do not** fasten off.

Fold Strap in half with RS facing each other (WS of last rnd will show). Join Strap by working 1 sl st lengthwise through tops of corresponding dc and foundation ch to end of row. Fasten off.

Sew Straps to WS at outer corners (see picture). BERNAT

Skill Levels

BEGINNER	Projects for first-time crocheters using basic stitches. Minimal shaping.
EASY	Projects using basic stitches, repetitive stitch patterns, simple color changes, simple shaping and finishing.
INTERMEDIATE	Projects with a variety of stitches and techniques. Crochet projects may involve basic lace patterns or color-patterns, mid-level shaping and finishing.
EXPERIENCED	Projects using advanced techniques. Crochet projects may involve non repeating patterns, multi-color techniques, fine threads, small hooks, detailed shaping and refined finishing.

DIAGRAM

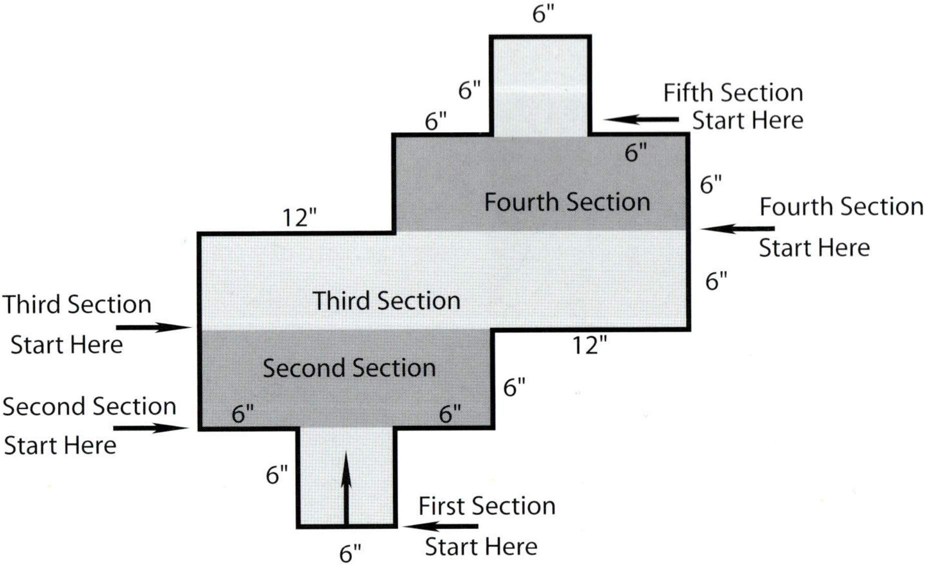

ASSEMBLY DIAGRAM

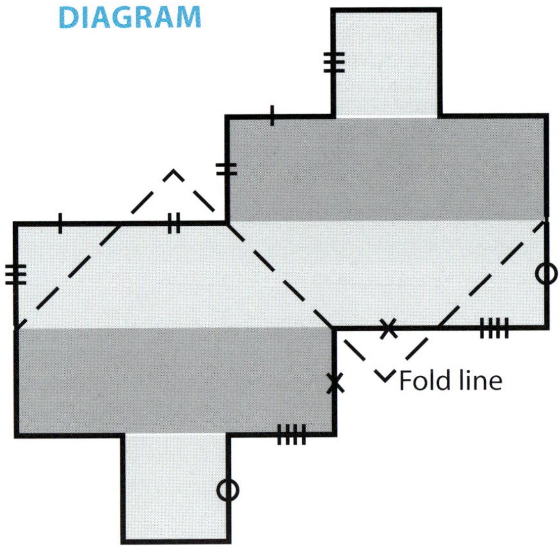

7. Rich Textures Tote (crochet)

4 MEDIUM

INTERMEDIATE

MEASUREMENTS

Approx 27" [68.5 cm] around x 19" [48 cm] high, excluding handles.

GAUGE

13 sc and 14 rows = 4" [10 cm].

MATERIALS

Bernat® Handicrafter® Cotton (50 g/1.75 oz; 73 m/80 yds)		
 Indigo (13114)	**8 balls**	**530 m/585 yds**
Size 5 mm (U.S. H/8) crochet hook **or size needed to obtain gauge.**		

ABBREVIATIONS

See page 41 for Helpful Hints

Approx = Approximately
Beg = Beginning
Bobble Cluster = [(Yoh and draw up a loop) 3 times. Yoh and draw through 6 loops on hook. Yoh and draw through 2 loops on hook – bobble made. Ch 2. Bobble] all in next st.
Ch = Chain(s)
Dc = Double crochet
Dcfp = Yoh and draw up a loop around post of next stitch at front of work inserting hook from right to left. (Yoh and draw through 2 loops on hook) twice.
Rem = Remaining
Rnd(s) = Round(s)
RS = Right side
Sc = Single crochet
Sl st = Slip stitch
Sp(s) = Space(s)
St(s) = Stitch(es)
Tog = Together
WS = Wrong side
Yoh = Yarn over hook

INSTRUCTIONS

BAG

(See Charts VI and VII on pages 36 and 37).

Note: Ch 2 at beg of rnd **does not** count as st.

Ch 4. Join with sl st in first ch to form ring.

1st rnd: Ch 3 (counts as dc). 7 dc in ring. Join with sl st to top of ch 3. 8 dc.

2nd rnd: Ch 2. 1 dcfp around first dc. 1 dc in sp between last dc and next dc. (1 dcfp around next dc. 1 dc in sp between last dc and next dc) 7 times. Join with sl st to first dcfp. 16 sts.

3rd rnd: Ch 2. 1 dcfp around first dcfp. Ch 2. 1 sc in next dc. Ch 2. (1 dcfp around next dcfp. Ch 2. 1 sc in next dc. Ch 2) 7 times. Join with sl st to first dcfp.

4th rnd: Ch 2. 2 dcfp around first dcfp. Ch 1. Bobble Cluster in next sc. Ch 1. (2 dcfp around next dcfp. Ch 1. Bobble Cluster in next sc. Ch 1) 7 times. Join with sl st to first dcfp.

5th rnd: Ch 2. 2 dcfp around each of first 2 dcfp. Ch 1. Bobble Cluster in next ch-2 sp. Ch 1. (2 dcfp around each of next 2 dcfp. Ch 1. Bobble Cluster in next ch-2 sp. Ch 1) 7 times. Join with sl st to first dcfp.

6th rnd: Ch 2. 2 dcfp around first dcfp. 1 dcfp around each of next 3 dcfp. Ch 1. Bobble Cluster in next ch-2 sp. Ch 1. (2 dcfp around next dcfp. 1 dcfp around each of next 3 dcfp. Ch 1. Bobble Cluster in next ch-2 sp. Ch 1) 7 times. Join with sl st to first dcfp.

7th rnd: Ch 2. 2 dcfp around first dcfp. 1 dcfp around each of next 4 dcfp. Ch 1. Bobble Cluster in next ch-2 sp. Ch 1. (2 dcfp around next dcfp. 1 dcfp around each of next 4 dcfp. Ch 1. Bobble Cluster in next ch-2 sp. Ch 1) 7 times. Join with sl st to first dcfp.

8th rnd: Ch 2. 1 dcfp around each of first 3 dcfp. Ch 2. 1 dcfp around each of next 3 dcfp. Ch 2. 1 sc in next ch-2 sp. Ch 2. (1 dcfp around each of next 3 dcfp. Ch 2. 1 dcfp around each of next 3 dcfp. Ch 2. 1 sc in next ch-2 sp. Ch 2) 7 times. Join with sl st to first dcfp.

9th rnd: Ch 2. (1 dcfp around each of next 3 dcfp. Ch 2. 1 sc in next ch-2 sp. Ch 2. 1 dcfp around each of next 3 dcfp. Ch 2. Miss next ch-2 sp, sc, ch-2 sp) 8 times. Join with sl st to first dcfp.

10th rnd: Ch 2. (1 dcfp around each of next 3 dcfp. Ch 1. Bobble Cluster in next sc. Ch 1. 1 dcfp around each of next 3 dcfp. Miss next ch-2 sp) 8 times. Join with sl st to first dcfp.

11th to 13th rnds: Ch 2. (1 dcfp around each of next 3 dcfp. Ch 1. Bobble Cluster in next ch-2 sp. Ch 1. 1 dcfp around each of next 3 dcfp) 8 times. Join with sl st to first dcfp.

14th rnd: Ch 2. (1 dcfp around each of next 3 dcfp. Ch 2. 1 sc in next ch-2 sp. Ch 2. 1 dcfp around each of next 3 dcfp. Ch 2) 8 times. Join with sl st to first st.

15th rnd: Ch 2. (1 dcfp around each of next 3 dcfp. Ch 2. Miss next ch-2 sp, sc, ch-2 sp. 1 dcfp around each of next 3 dcfp. Ch 2. 1 sc in next ch-2 sp. Ch 2) 8 times. Join with sl st to first st.

16th rnd: Ch 2. (1 dcfp around each of next 3 dcfp. Miss next ch-2 sp. 1 dcfp around each of next 3 dcfp. Ch 1. Bobble Cluster in next sc) 8 times. Join with sl st to first st.

17th to 19th rnds: Ch 2. (1 dcfp around each of next 6 dcfp. Ch 1. Bobble Cluster in next ch-2 sp. Ch 1) 8 times. Join with sl st to first st.

20th to 31st rnds: As 8th to 19th rnds.

32nd to 37th rnds: As 8th to 13th rnds.

38th rnd: Ch 2. (1 dcfp around each of next 3 dcfp. Ch 2. 1 sc in next ch-2 sp. Ch 2. 1 dcfp around each of next 3 dcfp) 8 times. Join with sl st to first st.

39th rnd: Ch 2. (1 dcfp around each of next 3 dcfp. Ch 2. Miss next ch 2, sc, ch 2. 1 dcfp around each of next 3 dcfp) 8 times. Join with sl st to first st.

40th rnd: Ch 2. (1 dcfp around each of next 3 dcfp. Miss next ch-2 sp. 1 dcfp around each of next 3 dcfp) 8 times. Join with sl st to first st.

41st and 42nd rnds: Ch 2. *1 dcfp around next dcfp. Rep from * around. Join with sl st to first st. 48 dcfp.

Fasten off.

Strap (make 2)

With 2 strands held tog, ch 84.

1st rnd: 1 dc in 4th ch from hook. 1 dc in each ch to end of ch. *Working into rem loops along opposite side of ch,* work 1 dc in each ch to end of chain. Ch 1. **Do not** fasten off.

Fold Strap in half lengthwise with RS facing each other (WS of last rnd will show). Join Strap by working 1 sl st through tops of corresponding dc and foundation ch to end of row. Fasten off.

Sew Straps to Bag as shown in picture. BERNAT

CHART VI

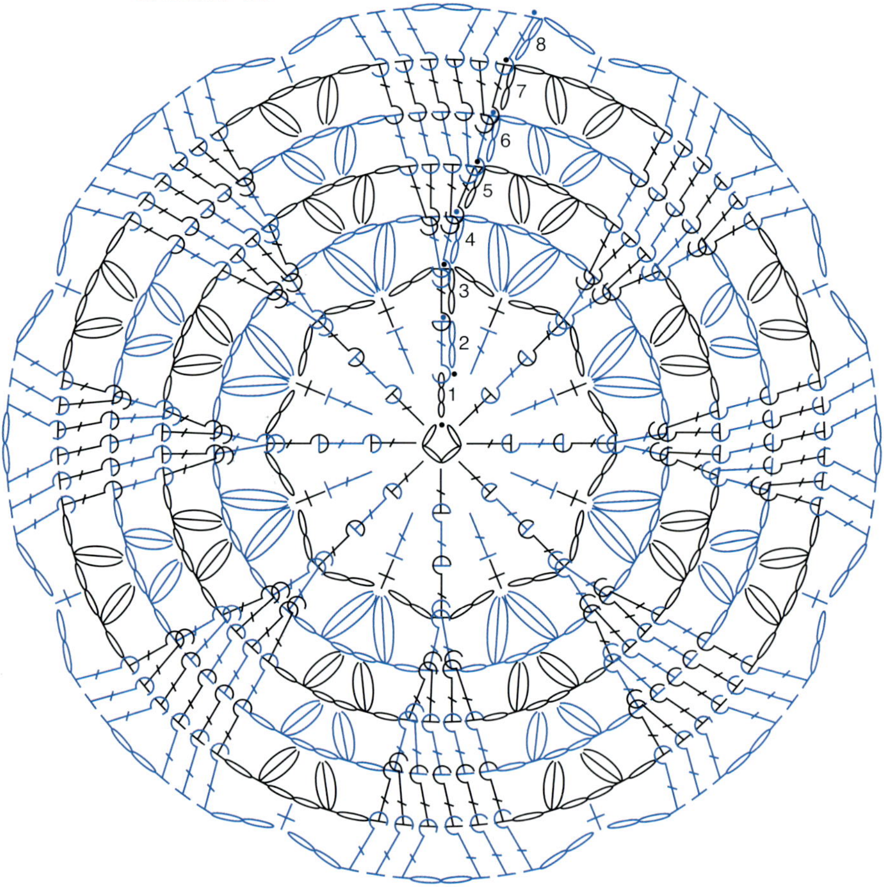

1st-8th RNDS

CHART VII

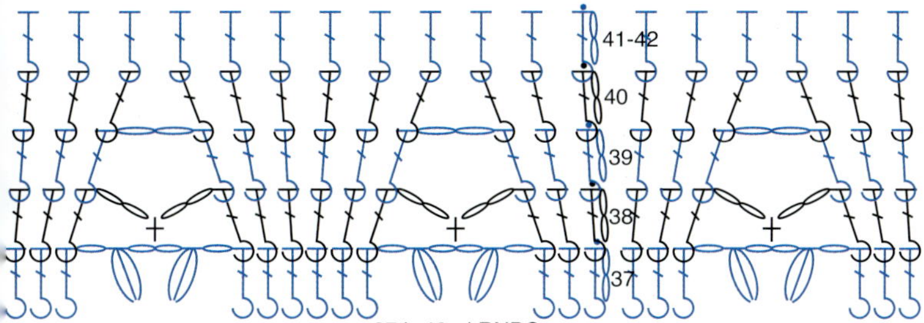

37th-42nd RNDS

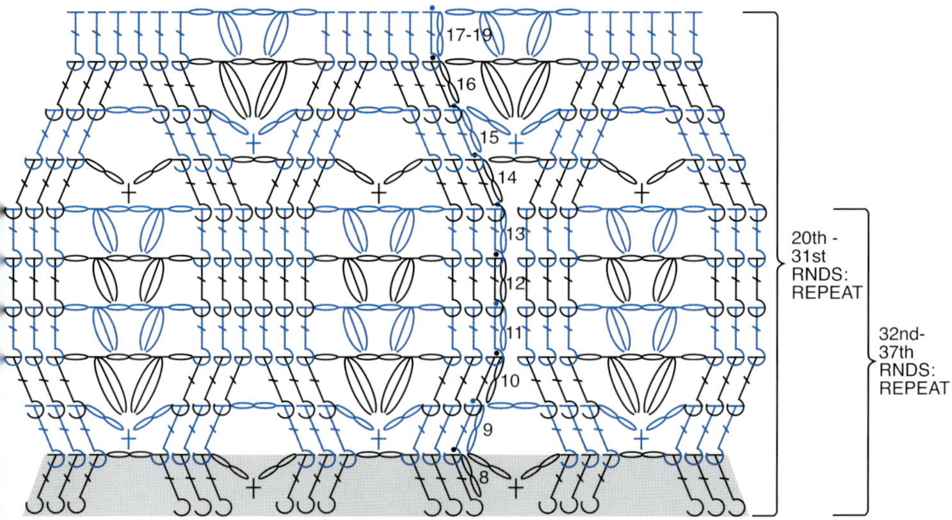

8th-19th RNDS

KEY

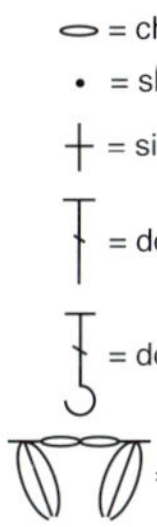

= chain (ch)

= slip st (sl st)

= single crochet (sc)

= double crochet (dc)

= double crochet front post (dcfp)

= Bobble Cluster

8. Totally Triangles! Multi-Use Bags (crochet)

4 MEDIUM

INTERMEDIATE

MEASUREMENTS

Version A: Approx 10" [25.5 cm] wide x 11" [28 cm] long.

Version B: Approx 10" [25.5 cm] wide x 5½" [14 cm] long.

GAUGE

13 sc and 14 rows = 4" [10 cm].

ABBREVIATIONS

See page 41 for Helpful Hints

Approx = Approximately
Beg = Beginning
Ch = Chain(s)
Cont = Continue
Rem = Remain(ing)
Rep = Repeat
Rnd(s) = Round(s)
Sc = Single crochet
Sl st = Slip stitch
St(s) = Stitch(es)
Tog = Together
WS = Wrong side

MATERIALS

Bernat® Handicrafter® Cotton
(50 g/1.75 oz; 73 m/80 yds)

Sizes	Version A	Version B
Main Color (MC) Off White (00002)	**2 balls or 118 m/128 yds**	**1 ball or 58 m/64 yds**
Contrast A Black Liquorice (13040)	**1 ball or 43 m/47 yds**	**1 ball or 23 m/25 yds**
Contrast B Robin's Egg (13215)	**1 ball or 31 m/34 yds**	**1 ball or 17 m/19 yds**
Contrast C Warm Brown (13130)	**1 ball or 26 m/29 yds**	**1 ball or 14 m/15 yds**
Contrast D Hot Purple (13317)	**1 ball or 35 m/39 yds**	**1 ball or 18 m/20 yds**
Contrast E Tangerine (13699)	**1 ball or 26 m/29 yds**	**1 ball or 14 m/15 yds**

Size 5 mm (U.S. H/8) crochet hook **or size needed to obtain gauge.**
Zipper 10" [25 cm] long for both Versions.

INSTRUCTIONS

Notes

- When joining new color, work to last 2 loops on hook of last st. Draw new color through 2 loops, then proceed in a new color. Carry color not in use across top of previous rnd and work sts around it to prevent stranding.
- Join with sl st at end of each rnd.

The instructions are written for smaller size. If changes are needed for larger size, the instructions will be written thus ( ).

With A, ch 33.

1st rnd: 1 sc in 2nd ch from hook. 1 sc in each ch to last ch. 3 sc in last ch. **Do not** turn. *Working in rem loops of foundation ch,* 1 sc in each ch to end of chain. Join with sl st to first sc. 65 sc.

2nd rnd: With A, ch 1. *1 sc in each of next 4 sc. With MC, 1 sc in next sc. Rep from * around. Join with sl st to first sc. 1st row of Chart VIII is complete.

Cont working Chart VIII in sc, *reading rows from **right** to left,* until Chart VIII has been worked 1 (2) time(s), ending on 20th row of Chart. Fasten off.

FINISHING

Sew zipper into bag at top edge. BERNAT

CHART VIII

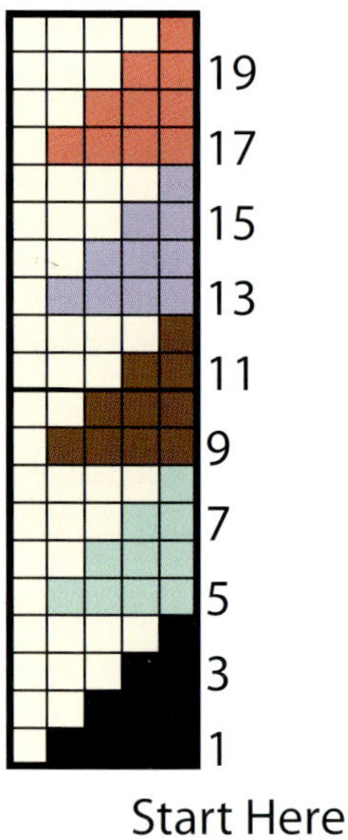

KEY

- □ = Main Color (MC)
- ■ = Contrast A
- ■ = Contrast B
- ■ = Contrast C
- ■ = Contrast D
- ■ = Contrast E

Helpful Hints

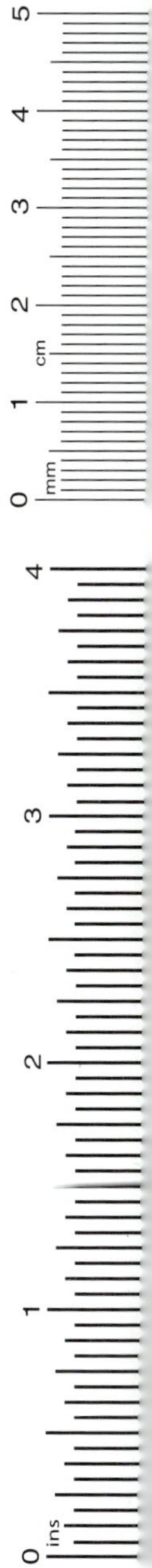

Bernat® Handicrafter® Cotton
Solids: 50 g/1.75 oz; 73 m/80 yds
Ombres & Prints: 42.5 g/1.5 oz; 62 m/68 yds
100% cotton

WASHING AND CARE INSTRUCTIONS

Machine wash or hand wash in cold water using a mild soap. Machine dry.

Machine Washing: Wash item, preferably on its own, using a delicate cycle, cool water and detergent. Softener may be added to the final rinse. **Do not** use bleach.

Machine Drying: Tumble dry at low heat setting. Do not overheat.

U.S. Knitters Please Note: Canadian and American terminologies differ slightly. Equivalents are shown.

Canadian	**U.S.**
cast off	bind off
tension	gauge

* = The star symbol is a repeat sign and means that you follow the printed instructions from the first * until you reach the second *. You will then repeat from * to * the given number of times which does not include the first time. The ** and *** are used in the same way.

ABBREVIATIONS: cm = centimeter(s), g = gram(s), " = inch(es), m = meter(s), mm = millimeter(s), oz = ounce(s), 0 = no stitches, times or rows

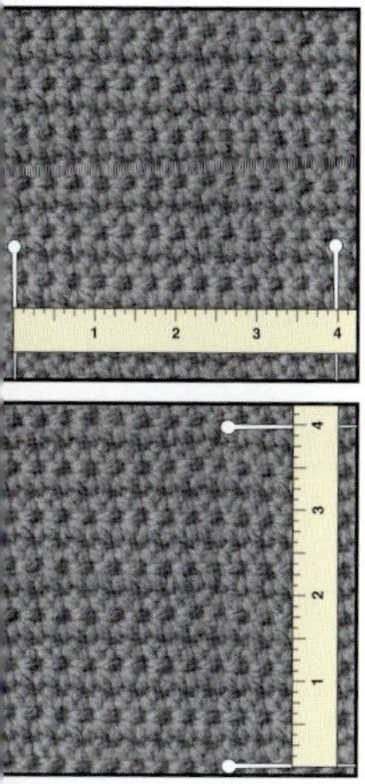

GAUGE SWATCH

For best results, be sure to use the yarn recommended in the pattern, and purchase enough of one dye lot to complete your project. It is a good idea to retain ball bands in case of inquiry. Before you begin to crochet, check your gauge by making a test swatch and adjusting your hook size, if necessary, to obtain the gauge quoted in the pattern. Inaccurate gauge results in an item too large or too small. Even a variation of half a stitch makes an obvious difference in the finished size.

(Example crochet gauge swatch shown: 12 sc and 13 rows).

Learn to Crochet Instructions

Slip Knot

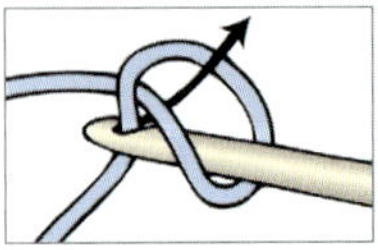

1 Make a loop, then hook another loop through it.

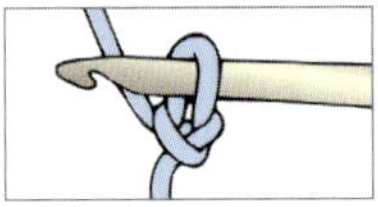

2 Tighten gently and slide the knot up to the hook.

Chain Stitch (ch)

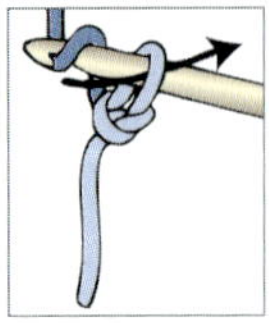

1 Yarn over hook (yoh) and draw the yarn through to form a new loop without tightening up the previous one.

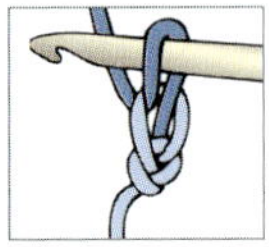

2 Repeat to form as many chains (ch) as required. Do not count the slip knot as a stitch.

Slip Stitch (sl st)

This is the shortest crochet stitch and unlike other stitches is not used on its own to produce a fabric. It is used for joining, shaping and where necessary carrying the yarn to another part of the fabric for the next stage.

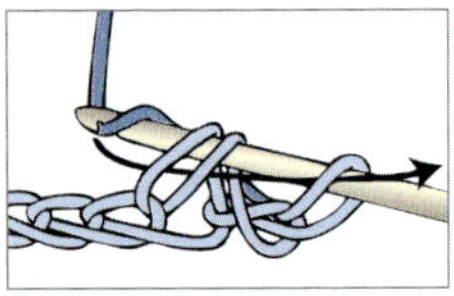

Insert hook into work (second chain from hook), yarn over hook (yoh) and draw the yarn through both the work and loop on hook in one movement.

To join a chain ring with a slip stitch (sl st), insert hook into first chain (ch), yarn over hook (yoh) and draw through both the work and the yarn on hook in one movement.

Single Crochet (sc)

1 Insert the hook into the work [2nd chain (ch) from hook on starting chain], *yarn over hook (yoh) and draw yarn through the work only.

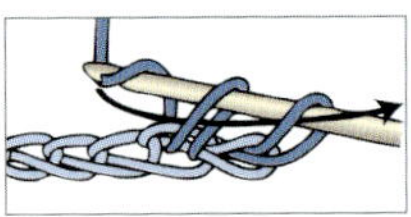

2 Yarn over hook (yoh) again and draw the yarn through both loops on the hook.

3 1 single crochet (sc) made. Insert hook into next stitch: repeat (rep) from * in step 1.